CLUE BOKS

Birds

Gwen Allen   Joan Denslow

OXFORD UNIVERSITY PRESS

Oxford University Press, Great Clarendon Street, Oxford OX2 6DP

Oxford New York Athens Auckland Bangkok Bogotá Bombay
Buenos Aires Calcutta Cape Town Dar es Salaam Delhi
Florence Hong Kong Istanbul Karachi Kuala Lumpur Madras
Madrid Melbourne Mexico City Nairobi Paris Singapore
Taipei Tokyo Toronto
and associated companies in Berlin and Ibadan

Oxford is a trade mark of Oxford University Press

© Oxford University Press 1997
First published 1970
New edition 1997

CLUE BOOKS – BIRDS
produced for Oxford University Press
by Bender Richardson White, Uxbridge

Editors: Lionel Bender, John Stidworthy Design: Ben White
Media Conversion and Page Make-up: MW Graphics
Project Manager: Kim Richardson
Colour plates: Richard Allen, Norman Arlott, Trevor Boyer, Hilary Burn,
P J·K Burton, C J F Coombs, N W Cusa, H Delin, Kim Franklin, Robert
Gillmor, Alan Harris, Peter Hayman, Mark Hulme, Miss C E Talbot Kelly,
Ian Lewington, Viggo Lee, Darren Rees, Chris Rose, Christopher Schmidt,
Sir Peter Scott, Laurel Tucker, D I M Wallace, Ian Willis, Dan Zetterström
Other artwork: E A R Ennion, Ron Hayward, Clive Pritchard

A CIP catalogue record for this book is available from the British Library

ISBN 0-19-910180-9 (hardback)   ISBN 0-19-910186-8 (paperback)

1 3 5 7 9 10 8 6 4 2

Printed in Italy

CONTENTS

ABOUT THIS BOOK

This book is about birds commonly seen in northern and western Europe.
It allows you to identify these birds and it tells you a little about their lifestyles
and habits.

The book is divided into three main sections: Introduction, Clues and
Identification. The Introduction section tells you the best way to watch and
study birds and to record your observations.

The Clues section allows you to identify each bird you have seen. Start on page
12 and follow the clues. The arrows and numbers in the right-hand margin or
next to illustrations tell you which page or pages to go to next.

The Identification Section consists of colour plates illustrating the individual
types or species of birds, arranged in related groups. Most of the birds you see
will be illustrated in this section. Alongside each illustration is a basic
description of the bird. Throughout the book, measurements are given in
centimetres or metres – abbreviated to cm or m (10 cm = approximately
4 inches)

The coloured band at the top of each double-page spread helps you locate
the relevant sections of the book: *blue* for Introduction, *yellow* for Clues,
red for Identification. An arrowhead at the top right of a page or spread shows
the topic continues on to the next page or spread. A bar at the top right
indicates the end of that topic.

PARTS OF A BIRD

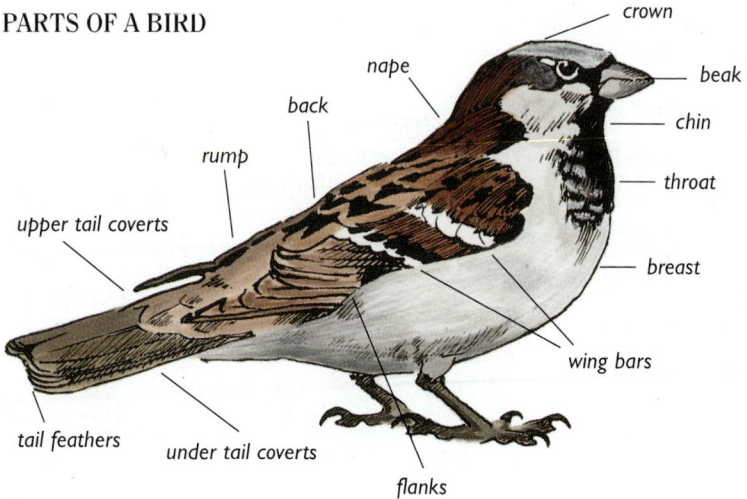

BIRD FAMILIES

Birds that are alike in shape and which behave in the same way belong to groups called families. Ducks and geese and swans all belong to the family ANATIDAE. Thrushes and blackbirds and robins belong to the family TURDIDAE. Ornithologists (people who study birds) have made up these family names from Latin words.

In each family group are different kinds of birds, or, as ornithologists say, different species. In the family TURDIDAE, the Blackbird belongs to one species, the Song Thrush to another and the Mistle Thrush to another. In the family PARIDAE, the Blue Tit belongs to one species, the Great Tit to another and the Coal Tit to a third.

PLUMAGE

The feathers of a bird are called its **PLUMAGE**. The cocks and hens (males and females) of some kinds of bird have plumage of different colours. Sometimes the young are different from their parents. Some birds have different coloured plumage in winter and summer.

Every year, usually in the autumn, a bird loses some of its feathers. This is called **MOULTING**.

tail feathers

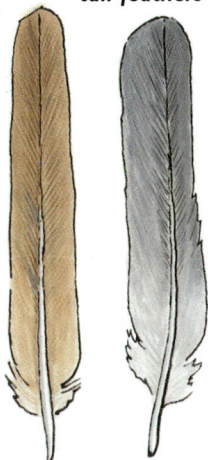

wing feathers

body feathers

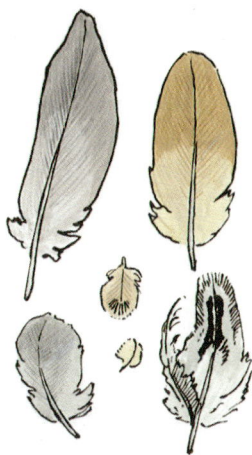

Collect feathers and mount them on stiff paper. Put together the feathers that look alike. When you have learned to recognise a lot of birds, see if you can decide which feathers come from which kind of bird.

Some feathers change colour when you look at them from different angles. Feathers like this are called **IRIDESCENT**.

SIZE

The size of each bird is given in centimetres in the captions by the illustrations on pages 34–79. As a guide, a House Sparrow is about 15 cm long, a Rook about 45 cm.

Rook to same scale as House Sparrow

You can watch birds of many different kinds in parks, woods and fields, by rivers and lakes and near the sea. You can also attract birds to your garden by putting out a variety of foods.

It is best to put food on a bird table; here the birds are safe from cats. You may like to make a table like the one in the picture below, or a simpler one made from a flat piece of wood or an old tray nailed to a post. The clues on pages 12–33 will help you to name the birds that come to the table.

Put out cheese rinds, seeds, berries, apple slices, bacon rind and bread. Hang nuts or scraps of food in a wire container or net nylon bag. Put fat in an empty coconut shell or hang suet from a string. If you have no bird table, all these containers can be hung from branches or posts.

A dish of water is very important.

Birds do not all behave in the same way. Each kind has its own pattern of behaviour.

Watch them carefully and record in a book what you have seen.
A book like this is called a **FIELD NOTEBOOK**.

Give each type of bird a different page.
At the top of the page write a description of the bird (see page 9) and stick in a picture of it (if you can find one). Then draw six columns and give them headings like this:

date	time of day	kind of weather	what the bird ate	what the bird did	was the bird alone?

Every time you see a bird at your table, record it in your book.

When you have been using your notebook for a few weeks, you will be able to answer questions like these:

How many different kinds of bird visited the table?
Which kind of bird visited the table most often?

and for each kind of bird:

In what sort of weather did it come most often?
At what time of day did it come most often?
Did it prefer any particular type of food?
Did it chase other birds away or threaten
them, and if so how?
Was it usually alone or with other birds
of the same kind?

Try to think of other questions to answer
about the birds that visit your table.

threat displays

Look for birds wherever you are, on a walk in the country, by a river or lake, by the sea, in your garden, in the park or at the zoo.

Write down in your field notebook descriptions of the birds you see and where you see them. You may not be able to see these birds as clearly as in the illustrations in this book, but try to make notes about:

the size of each bird
the shape of its body (see pages 24–33)
the shape of its beak (see pages 14–19)
the kind of feet and legs it has (see pages 20–23)
its colour
how it walks, hops or flies (see pages 24–29)
what it is doing
how it behaves with other birds

The parts of the bird named in the illustration on page 4 will help you to make records of the position of the various coloured parts.

Look for footprints in mud, sand and snow (see pages 10 and 11).

bird footprints

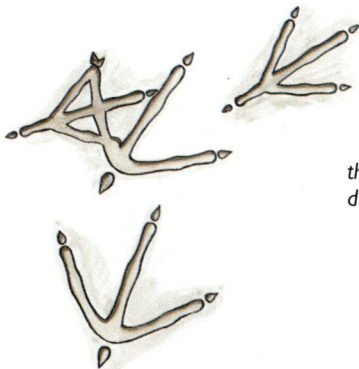

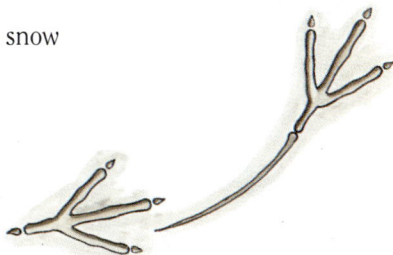

the long scratch is often made by a bird dragging its claw

You may find footprints in sand, mud or snow, or you can put a tray of wet sand or mud near the bird table. Measure the footprints and draw them life size in your field notebook.

If they show a long hind toe, they were probably made by perching birds (pages 34–53; 55–63). If they were arranged like this, the bird was hopping.

If they were arranged like this, the bird was running or walking.

If they have a short hind toe, or none, they were probably made by a wader (pages 76–77), or a pigeon (pages 62–63), or a game bird (pages 66–67) or a Moorhen (page 70).

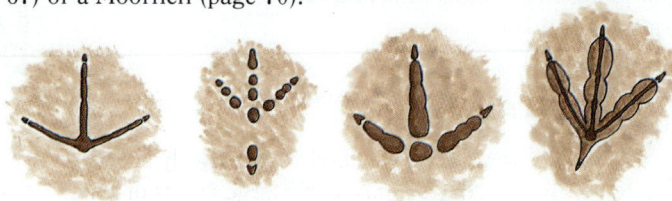

If the prints are this shape, they were made by a bird with a webbed foot (pages 68–69, 70, 72–75, 78–79). There is often only a tiny prick from the hind claw.

You can make a plaster cast of a footprint

You will need:
a small tin   some plaster of Paris
a stick for stirring   water
stiff paper   paint
paper clips   clear varnish
penknife

Put a strip of paper about 3 cm
wide around the footprint. Hold
the ends of the strip together
with a paper clip.

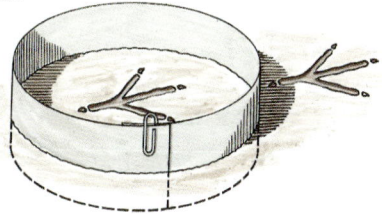

Decide how much water will be needed to fill the space surrounded by
the paper. Put a little less than this into the tin. Add plaster a little at a
time, keeping it well stirred, until the mixture is thick but can be
poured into the paper ring. Pour the mixture over the footprints and
make the top smooth. You will get used to the quantities when you
have done this several times.

Leave it to dry until it is hard; this should take about 10 minutes.

When it is hard, remove the paper and very carefully lever up the
plaster cast with a penknife. Remove any large pieces of mud.

When the cast is really hard, wash off
the rest of the mud with a soft
nailbrush or old toothbrush.

Paint the shape of the footprint,
and then varnish the whole cast
with clear varnish.

SIZE and BEAK SHAPE

CLUE A

If the bird is less than 30 cm long

➤ 14 –15

CLUE B

If the bird is more than 30 cm long and is seen on or near water

➤ 16 –17

CLUE C

If the bird is more than 30 cm long and seen away from water

➤ 18 –19

FEET and LEGS

CLUE D

If the foot has no web between the toes

➤ 20 –21

CLUE E

If the foot is webbed

➤ 22 –23

FOOTPRINTS

CLUE F | If you have found footprints

➡ 10 –11

SHAPES and MOVEMENT

CLUE G | If you have watched birds flying

➡ 24 –27

CLUE H | If you have watched birds on the ground

➡ 28 –29

CLUE I | If you have watched birds in trees

➡ 30 –31

CLUE J | If you have watched birds swimming

➡ 32 –33

SMALL BIRDS of sparrow size (15 cm or less)

CLUE **A** | If the bird has a stumpy beak, for cracking seeds

34 –39

CLUE **B** | If it has a small beak for picking insects and spiders out of cracks or eating nuts, and it often hangs upside down

40 50–52

CLUE **C** | If it has a short slender beak, for eating soft fruit, worms and insects

41 46–47

CLUE **D** | If it has a forked tail and a quick wheeling flight for catching insects in flight

54 55

SMALL BIRDS of Blackbird size (20 cm to 25 cm)

CLUE E   If it has a slender beak, for eating soft fruits and
small animals

➡ 48
–49,
55

if seen on the sea   ➡ 72

CLUE F   If it has a long,
strong beak for
pecking holes in wood

➡ 56
–57

CLUE G   If it has a hooked beak, for eating other birds and
small mammals

➡ 64
65

LARGE BIRDS more than 30 cm long

Usually seen near water

CLUE **A**   If it has a flat bill

68
78–79

CLUE **B**   If it has a short pointed beak

70

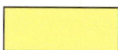
CLUE C | If it has a stout blunt beak

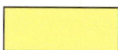 **73
–75
79**

CLUE D | If it has a long pointed beak and long legs

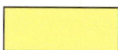 **79**

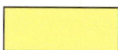 **76
–77**

LARGE BIRDS more than 30 cm long

Usually seen away from water

CLUE A   If it has a pointed beak and crest

➡ **76**

CLUE B   If it has a stout beak

➡ **58 –63**

CLUE C | If it has a long strong beak

→ 56

CLUE D | If it has a very short beak

→ 66

CLUE E | If it has a hooked beak

→ 64

FEET

It is sometimes possible to find the feet of dead birds; these can be mounted and kept for closer observation.

CLUE A

If the foot has three toes in front and one strong toe behind and if the bird lives where there are trees and bushes, it belongs to one of the perching birds.

34
–53
55
58–61

CLUE B

If it has two toes forwards and two behind, it belongs either to a **CUCKOO** or a **WOODPECKER** – the outer toe can turn forwards or backwards.

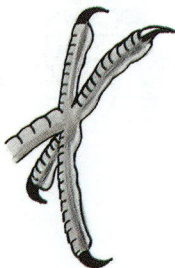

56
–58

CLUE C

If it has four toes pointing forwards, it belongs to a **SWIFT**.

→ 55

CLUE D

If it has hooked toes, called talons, it belongs to a **BIRD OF PREY**.

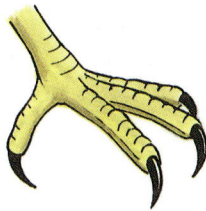

→ 64 –65

CLUE E

If the foot has three toes in front and one smaller toe behind and if the bird lives near water, it probably belongs to one of the wading birds or a **MOORHEN**; if on land, to a game bird or **PIGEON**.

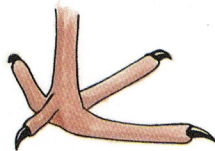

→ 62 –63 66–67 70–71 76–79

CLUE A

If the foot is fully webbed round three toes, it belongs to a **GULL** or **DUCK**.

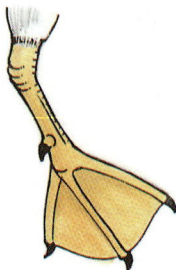

68
–69
73–75

CLUE B

If the foot is only three-quarters webbed round three toes, it belongs to a **TERN**.

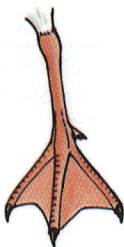

72

CLUE C

If the foot is webbed and very large, it belongs to a **GOOSE** or a **SWAN**.

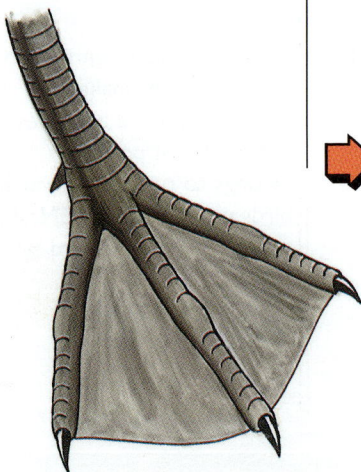

78
–79

CLUE D

If all four toes are in the web, the foot belongs to the **CORMORANT** family of birds.

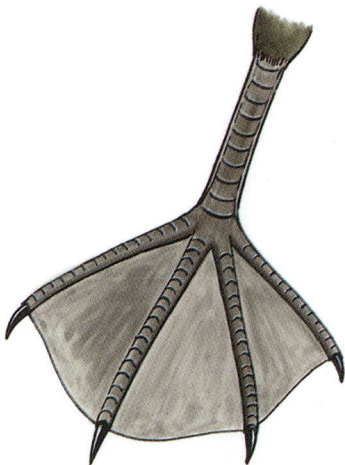

➡ 79

CLUE E

If the foot has lobes, it belongs to a **COOT**.

➡ 70

Dotted lines show flight paths

CLUE A

Flies high in
circles singing

41

CLUE B

Quick, wheeling
flight

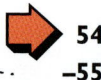

54
–55

CLUE C

Many small birds have
a bounding flight

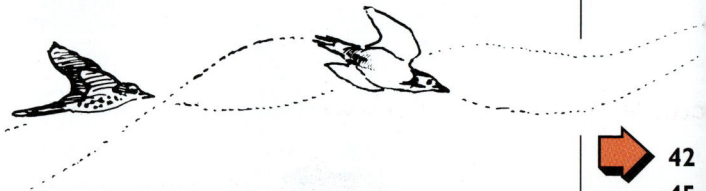

42
–45
48
56–57

CLUE D | Undulating flight. Short jump flights to catch flies

➤ **48**

CLUE E | Straight twinkling flight and star silhouette

➤ **45**

CLUE F | Bouncing flight, wings half-closed going down

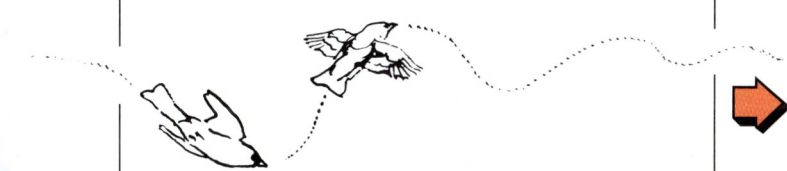

➤ **34 −39**

CLUE G | Very small birds with jerky flight high up

➤ **50**

CLUE H | Straight flight, low down

➤ **40**

CLUE I | Brightly coloured bird near water

➤ **55**

Dotted lines show speed and depth of wing beats

CLUE A Fast twinkling beats; neck out
68

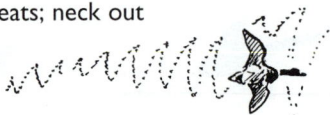

CLUE B Very big birds; neck out; steady beats
78

Neck folded; very slow beats
79

CLUE C Slow irregular beats; often glides
73 −75

CLUE D Hovers and glides
65

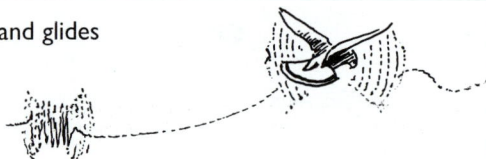

CLUE E Fairly fast regular beats
79

CLUE F Flight fast and direct
62 −63

CLUE G | Slow easy flaps and glides

→ 59
60–61

CLUE H | Level mechanical flight

→ 58

CLUE I | Unsteady floppy flight

→ 59

CLUE J | Fast whirring beats between glides

→ 66

CLUE K | Low, slow and wavering

→ 64

CLUE L | Low weak flight to cover

→ 70

CLUE A Long tail, walks quickly, sometimes runs

66

CLUE B Walks or runs short distance, then stops and picks up morsel with beak. Crested bird on moor or farmland.

76

CLUE C Walking constantly probing ground or picking at shellfish. May be a wading bird.

77

CLUE D Hops, often many of these birds together.

38

CLUE E Waddling and hopping, prodding at lawns etc. with beak

45

CLUE F Long narrow toes, walks well, flicks tail up

➤ 70 –71

CLUE G Short tail, may walk and run with body low and hunched ➤ 66

CLUE H
Long, lobed toes but walking and running well

➤ 70

CLUE I Large dark bird, walking with a waddle ➤ 60 –61

CLUE J Runs a short distance, then stops with body upright, watching and listening for food. Seen in garden

➤ 42

CLUE K Runs, with very long hind claws. Seen in open country

➤ 41

Look for shapes, patterns, and angle the birds perch at

CLUE A

65

62

58

56

CLUE B Climbs upwards only, using tail as a prop

CLUE **C**

→ 59

CLUE **E**

CLUE **D**

→ 60

→ 60

CLUE **F**

→ 52

CLUE **G**

→ 50

Runs both up and down
trunk, tail free

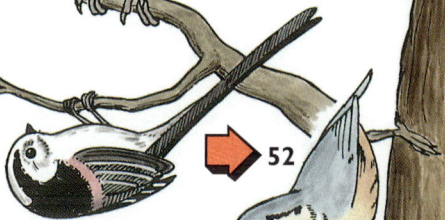

→ 40

CLUE **H**

CLUE **I**

→ 64

CLUE A | Swims low far out

➡ 79

CLUE B | Sharp wings; forked tail; splash-dives from air

➡ 72

CLUE C | Up-ends

➡ 68

CLUE D | Wades near shore; does not normally swim

➡ 76 –77

CLUE E Swims high; long bent wings

73 –75

CLUE F Tail low

70

CLUE G Tail high

70

CLUE H Jumps to dive in open water

68

CLUE I Long tail; runs or paddles by shore

48

male

female

Greenfinch
(14 cm)

Powerful head and bill for size. In farmland, parks and gardens, in pairs or small flocks. Often comes to bird tables. Vocal, with twittering calls, or a long, nasal drone. Nest an untidy cup of grass and roots in a hedge or tree, often near others. Eats seeds and berries.

male

female

Chaffinch
(15 cm)

Found in woods, parks and gardens. In winter, may form large flocks, sometimes with other small birds. Call a loud 'spink, spink'. Nests in hedge or tree, making cup nest of moss and lichens. Feeds on ground on seeds and collects some insect food from trees.

male

female

Brambling
(15 cm)

Breeds in northern Europe, and is a winter visitor to Britain. In winter the male's head and back are mottled brown, with white rump. Forms large flocks in winter, which feed on beech mast and on seeds in stubble fields, often alongside Chaffinches.

female

male

Siskin
(12 cm)

Mainly a bird of conifer forests, but in winter visits other types of wood and gardens. Behaves like a tit; call a constant twittering. Makes neat nest of twigs, lichens and moss at end of a branch high in a conifer tree. Eats seeds of conifers, and some insects.

Goldfinch
(12 cm)
Found on cultivated land, open woods,
hedgerows, parks and gardens. Neat nest of
rootlets, grass and moss built by female on
end of a branch. Outside breeding season
often in small flocks, sometimes with other
finches. Twitters during its undulating flight.
Eats seeds of thistle, dandelion, burdock
and other weeds, climbing acrobatically
over them.

male

female

Bullfinch
(15 cm)
Usually in pairs. Rather shy. Call a soft whistle. Nests in thick cover, such as
a thorn bush. Female builds nest of twigs, moss and lichen. Eats some tree
buds in late winter, so unpopular with fruit growers, but also eats tree seeds,
berries, weeds, and seeds of thistles and violets.

Hawfinch

(18 cm)

Heavily built, with a large bill for its size. Wary, and difficult to see, as it spends most of its time in the tree tops of broad-leaved woodland. Untidy nest made high in tree. Powerful bill able to crack open cherry stones. Feeds on large seeds, fruit stones, beech mast, and, as name suggests, haws.

male

female

Linnet

(13 cm)

Likes heathland and downland with scattered bushes. In winter may be seen with other finches feeding on farmland. Usually low in a bush, the nest is a strong construction of grass and moss. Often nests near other Linnets. Eats weed seeds.

male

female

House Sparrow
(15 cm)
In towns, villages and farms, rarely in open country away from buildings.
Lives in flocks, which are noisy and sometimes quarrelsome. Builds untidy
nest of straw or dry grass in hole almost anywhere in or around buildings.
Chirps constantly. Eats seeds, insects, scraps, bread, almost anything edible.

Tree Sparrow
(14 cm)
Sexes similar. Flocks are found in
cultivated areas with trees, not
much in towns, but sometimes
mixes with House Sparrows. Usually
nests in tree hole, making nest of
dry grass. Shriller voice than House
Sparrow. Eats seeds.

female

Yellowhammer
(16 cm)
Found in hedges, fields, and woodland edges. Rarely comes in gardens. Males may be seen and heard singing from the tops of hedges. Birds seen in ones and twos in summer, but in flocks in winter. Nest of grass and moss is made on or near the ground in a hedge-bottom. Call a rapid chip-chip-chip and long trill. Eats mainly seeds and insects in summer.

male

Reed Bunting
(15 cm)
Lives in reed beds and swamps. Sometimes seen on farmland in winter. Nest of grass, usually in a tussock on the ground. Males sometimes have several mates. Eat seeds of water plants in winter; also snails and insects in summer.

male

female

Wren
(10 cm)
Typically found in woods and gardens with thick undergrowth, but exists in all kinds of country. In spite of size, has a loud, shrill song and noisy alarm call. Male builds domed nest of moss, grass and leaves, often in a hole. Eats small insects, spiders, worms, woodlice and centipedes.

Treecreeper
(13 cm)
Lives in woods, also in parks and large gardens. Runs up tree trunks searching for food, then flies to base of next tree to climb again. Call a thin high note. Nest of grass and rootlets is made in crevice in bark. Eats small animals such as spiders and insects found in cracks in tree trunks.

Skylark
(18 cm)
In open country, both cultivated and uncultivated. Flies up almost vertically and sings as it goes. The varied trilling song can go on for five minutes. Nest a cup of grass on the ground. Eats weed seeds, some leaves, and also worms, spiders and insects.

Wheatear
(15 cm)
Summer visitor. Likes open hillsides, heathland and coastal areas. Call a hard 'chack'. A distinctive white rump is seen as it flits restlessly across open ground. Nest of grass and moss is made in a rock crevice or burrow. Mainly eats insects, and some other small animals such as spiders.

male

female

Song Thrush
(23 cm)
Lives in woods, parks and gardens. Song repeats each phrase.
Nest of dry grass with a lining of mud is made in a hedge or bush. Eats insects, worms, seeds, berries and fruits, and especially snails, which it often smashes on a special 'anvil stone'.

Mistle Thrush
(27 cm)
In many types of country, but mainly woodlands in summer. Flocks gather in open country in winter. Sings even in the roughest weather. The cup nest of grass and twigs is usually in a tree. Eats berries, including mistletoe, other fruit, insects, worms and snails.

Fieldfare
(25 cm)
Breeds in northern Europe. Visits Britain and southern Europe in winter. Large, chattering flocks may be seen feeding in the fields. It eats fruit and berries, also worms, snails, beetles and other insects.

Redwing
(21 cm)
Breeds in northern Europe. Visits Britain and southern Europe in winter. Chattering may be heard during night migration. Lives in flocks outside the breeding season, and often associates with Fieldfares on farmland and grassland. Eats worms, snails, insects, berries and fruit.

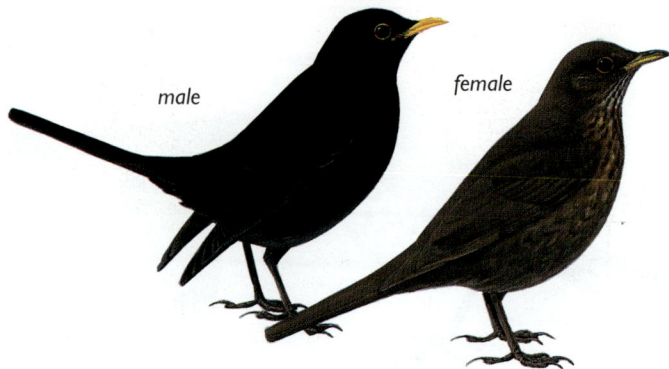

male *female*

Blackbird
(25 cm)
A bird of woodland glades that has found gardens and parks a good substitute. Often crashes noisily in undergrowth as it searches for food on the ground. Raises its tail as it alights. Pleasant song. Nest is a cup of mud, dry grass and leaves in bush or hedge. Eats worms, insects, some fruit and seeds.

male *juvenile*

Ring Ouzel
(24 cm)
Found in hills and mountains of Europe and Britain. Summer visitor above 300 m in the breeding season. Occasionally seen elsewhere as it migrates to Africa. Wary, keeps away from humans. Nest of heather and grass built on ground. Eats insects, worms and mountain berries.

summer  *winter*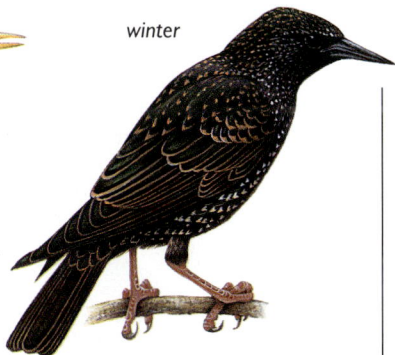

Starling
(22 cm)
In many types of country. Especially common near towns. Gregarious birds
that roost in enormous flocks enlarged by winter visitors; may be a huge
nuisance in town or country. Varied song. A good mimic. Nest of straw in
tree hole or on ledge. Eats pest insects such as leatherjackets, also worms,
spiders, slugs and various fruits.

 *male* *female*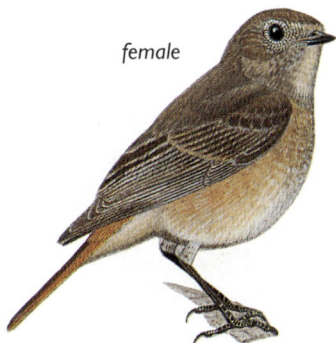

Redstart
(14 cm)
Summer visitor. Jerks tail. Lives in parks, gardens and open woodland. Female
builds nest of grass in a hole in tree, wall or bank. Eats mainly insects, also
some berries, spiders, and worms.

Robin
(14 cm)
Well-known garden bird, but also found in woodland and other types of country. Male often sings from a prominent perch to protect his territory. Nest is made in holes in trees or banks, or sometimes in a man-made object. Feeds on insects, worms, fruit and seeds.

adult

juvenile

Whinchat
(13 cm)
Summer visitor. Found on open heaths and scrubland, sometimes on farmland. Often perches on top of small bush. Nests on ground in rough grass. Eats spiders, worms, insects and their larvae.

male

female

male

Dunnock
(15 cm)
Prefers gardens and woodlands, but
sometimes in other types of
country. Thin high song, and call is a
shrill trill, but otherwise the bird
does not draw attention. It hops
quietly around searching for food. Its
nest is a cup of twigs and moss in a
bush or hedge. Eats insects and
other small animals, also small seeds.

female

Nightingale
(17 cm)
Summer visitor to southern England and Wales. Lives in thickets and thick
undergrowth in woods and swamps. Inconspicuous and shy, so rarely seen,
but has loud melodious song both day and night. Nest in undergrowth low
down or on ground. Eats on the ground, insects, worms and some berries.

adult

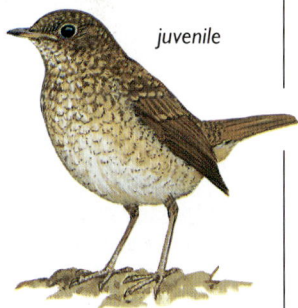

juvenile

Pied Wagtail and White Wagtail
(18 cm)

Pied and White Wagtails are same species in different geographical areas. Pied Wagtail is British variety; White Wagtail lives in mainland Europe, only occasionally seen in Britain as spring migrant. Spring plumage of males of each sub-species is very different. Pied Wagtail has a black back, while White Wagtail's back is much paler. Both wag their tails and bob their heads as they run. Both live on farmland, in open country, by water or in towns. Sometimes hundreds roost together, for example on the roof of a supermarket. Use hole in wall or bank for nest, lining it with hair and feathers. Feed on ground, but also make short, jumping flights to catch insects.

male Pied Wagtail

male White Wagtail

female

Grey Wagtail
(17 cm)

Often mistaken for Yellow Wagtail, but can be seen all year round near shallow water and streams. Can be either resident or migrant.

male

Yellow Wagtail
(17 cm)
Summer visitor. On the continental mainland, darker-headed varieties of males occur. Lives in water meadows, sewage farms, marshes and damp open areas. May follow cattle to search for food. Nests in hollow on ground. Eats flies and other insects.

juvenile

adult

juvenile

Spotted Flycatcher
(14 cm)
Summer visitor. Lives in parks, gardens and open woods. A quiet bird. Sits still on a perch by an open space, then swoops out to catch an insect, returning to the same perch. Makes an untidy nest of moss and hair on a ledge or in creepers. Eats flying insects.

Blue Tit
(11 cm)
Woodland bird, also very common in gardens. Searches for food on tree branches and trunks. Nests in tree hole. Eats small insects such as aphids and caterpillars.

Great Tit
(14 cm)
In woods, parks and gardens. May search for food low down or on ground. Takes nuts to a perch, holds them in its foot, pecks a hole in the shell and removes the contents. Great variety of calls. Nests in tree hole. Eats caterpillars and other insects, some seeds, nuts, buds and fruit.

Marsh Tit
(11 cm)
Seen in broad-leaved woodland with undergrowth, not particularly in marshes. Nests in hole. Feeds on insects, some seeds and berries. May hoard winter stores in autumn.

Coal Tit
(11 cm)
Lives in woodland with conifers. Searches for insects and their eggs among needles and bark, and also eats conifer seeds. Nests in holes low down.

Crested Tit
(11 cm)
Usually in pine woods, but seen in mixed woods too. In Britain it is confined to forests in parts of the Scottish Highlands. Call a soft churring sound. Nests in hole, or makes one in rotten wood. Eats caterpillars, aphids and other small insects from the tops of pine trees, and some pine seeds.

male

Bearded Tit
(17 cm)
Looks like a tit, but related to thrushes. Lives in reed-beds in swamps or at the edge of lakes and rivers. Climbs jerkily on reeds. Call a hard 'ping ping'. An open nest of reeds built near the ground. Eats insects, especially beetles, and reed seeds in winter.

female

Long-tailed Tit
(14 cm)
In woods, thickets, gardens and parks. Often in pairs or family parties. Soft piping calls. Nest, with a domed roof, is made in bush or tree fork, of moss, cobwebs and hair, covered in lichen and lined with feathers. Eats spiders, insects, seeds.

This variety is common in some parts of Europe

This is the variety seen in Britain

Nuthatch
(14 cm)
In woods with tall broad-leaved trees, parks and gardens. Runs up and down trees head first. Wedges nuts in crevices, then hammers them with bill. Nests in tree hole. Eats many insects, also hazel nuts, acorns, beech mast.

Goldcrest
(9 cm)
Smallest European bird. In woodland, especially in conifers. Busy, moving about tree tops. Thin high call. Builds open nest of moss, cobwebs and feathers, suspended like a hammock. Eats insects and spiders.

Willow Warbler
(11 cm)
Summer visitor. In open woods with thick undergrowth, bushy places and gardens. Always on the move. Plaintive call, fluent song of descending notes. The Chiff-chaff looks very similar, but it arrives earlier in the year and has a distinctive 'chiff-chaff' song. Domed nest usually built on ground. Eats small insects.

Blackcap
(14 cm)
Mainly summer visitor, some stay for winter. Likes woods, gardens and heathland with plenty of cover. Clear, strong song. The Garden Warbler looks and sounds similar, but its song is longer and quieter. Female makes light nest of grass and stems slung as a hammock. Eats caterpillars, flies, other insects and some berries.

male

female

Swallow
(19 cm)
Summer visitor. Long forked tail.
Red forehead and throat. Open
country, including cultivated
areas. Often flies over water,
catching insects. Builds open
cup nest of mud and grass
on a ledge, often in
barn or outbuilding.

House Martin
(13 cm)
Summer visitor. White
rump shows in flight.
Short forked tail. Often in large
flocks. Nests made from mud, grass
and saliva, with a small entrance,
placed under eaves of houses.
Eats insects caught on the wing.
Like Swallow, perches on wires.
Large flocks gather before migration.

Sand Martin
(12 cm)
Summer visitor. Often over
water, where it catches gnats and
other small insects. Lives in
colonies. Nests in a tunnel up to
90 cm long, made in sandbanks,
cliffs and gravel pits.

Swift
(17 cm)
Summer visitor. Except at the nest, is always in the air, even sleeping while flying. Flies fast, often in small flocks, screaming as it pursues insects. May be high in sky, or low near houses on summer evenings. Nests under eaves of buildings or on cliffs.

adult feeding young at nest

Kingfisher
(17 cm)
By rivers and streams, sometimes ponds. Large head and bill adapted for seizing fish. Sits still on perch before diving on prey. Sometimes hovers, but flight usually fast, low and straight, seen as a streak of vivid blue. Nests in burrow in riverbank. Eats small fish such as minnows and sticklebacks.

male

female

Green Woodpecker
(31 cm)
Red cheek stripe in male only. Young have red crown and red at base of bill; body speckled and barred. In woodlands with clearings, heaths, also parks and gardens. Often feeds on ground, opening nests of ants and licking them up. Also drills in trees for insect larvae. Bores hole in tree for nest. Laughing cry, giving its alternative
name of 'yaffle'.

male

female

Great Spotted Woodpecker
(23 cm)
Red on back of head in male only. Young have red crown and under-tail coverts. In all kinds of wooded places. Feeds mainly in trees, on beetle larvae and other wood-boring insects. Has no song. Instead, drums on trees fast and loud. Nest bored in
tree trunk.

male

female

female

Lesser Spotted Woodpecker
(15 cm)
Red crown in male, white in female.
Young have some crimson on crown
only; under-tail coverts brownish;
back and wings barred black and
white. Sparrow-sized and not very
common in Britain, where it is just
found in the south. Nests in hole
made in decayed wood. Feeds high
in broad-leaved trees, on insect
larvae and other small animals.

male

juvenile

Cuckoo
(33 cm)
Summer visitor. In all kinds of country. Male makes familiar 'cuckoo' call, female a trilling sound. Makes no nest. Female lays eggs in nests of other small birds, which rear the young Cuckoo that hatches. Eats insects, especially caterpillars, including some distasteful to other animals. Parents migrate in autumn, before the young.

Nightjar
(27 cm)
In woodlands with clearings, and on heathland. Rarely seen in day, as well-camouflaged and hidden, either on the ground or resting along a branch. Sometimes seen at dusk, twisting on long wings as it pursues flying insects. Churring song also heard after dark. Nests on ground.

Jay
(35 cm)

In woodlands and parks. Loud screeching 'skaark, skaark' call often gives away that it is about. Nest of twigs made in bush or tree. Eats insects, eggs, young birds and other small animals. Also fond of acorns, which it carries away and buries.

Magpie
(45 cm)

In farmland with trees, parkland and gardens. Seen alone, in pairs or in small groups. Nest a large collection of sticks with a domed roof, in tall trees. Eats insects, eggs and young of birds, seeds and fruit.

Jackdaw
(33 cm)
Around woods, fields, cliffs and even buildings. Strong, acrobatic flier. Often in flocks with other types of bird. Nest a pile of sticks. Nests built in colonies on cliffs, ruined buildings or in chimneys. Call a 'tchak'. Eats all kinds of food, from insects and other small animals to grain, fruit and carrion.

Carrion crow

Crow
(47 cm)
Two colour varieties: Carrion Crow, all black, found over most of western Europe, including Britain; Hooded Crow, with grey back and underparts, found in eastern, southern and northern Europe, including the Highlands of Scotland. Usually one or two together only. Lives in farmland, moors, and some built-up areas. Big nest of sticks. Eats grain, fruit, insects, eggs, small animals and carrion.

Hooded crow

Raven
(64 cm)
All black. Massive bill and wedge-shaped tail. Absent from heavily farmed areas, but found on moors, cliffs and wild places. Voice a deep croak. Stick nest built on ledge. Eats carrion, small animals, seeds and fruit.

Rook
(46 cm)
Bare face patch (in adult), slender bill and loose thigh feathers. Usually in large flocks. Lives in farmland with trees. Makes stick nests in treetop colonies. Eats worms, snails, insects, including many pests, fruit, seeds and carrion.

Chough
(38 cm)
Found on cliffs along western coasts of Britain and Ireland. Strong, acrobatic flyer, good at soaring. Nests in holes in rock faces. Eats insects and carrion.

Woodpigeon
(41 cm)
In farmland, woods, parks and gardens. In winter may be in huge flocks. Flies fast but takes off noisily. Nests in late summer, making a thin platform of twigs. Eats grain, other farm crops, seeds, acorns and fruit. Young birds ('squabs') are fed on 'pigeon's milk', from parent's mouth.

Collared Dove
(31 cm)
In parks, gardens and farmland. First bred in Britain in 1955, now common and becoming even more numerous. Call – a three-part coo with the second part emphasised – is often mistaken for an early Cuckoo. Flat nest of twigs. Eats grain and other seeds.

Rock Dove
(33 cm)
The ancestor of Domestic and Feral Pigeons.
Colouring blue grey, paler back and distinct
white rump; colours of domestic varieties
are very varied. The song is like the
Domestic Pigeon. Lives around
rocky cliffs, mostly in Scotland
and Ireland. Nests are built
in rock crevices and caves.

Feral Pigeon
(33 cm)
The same species of bird as the Rock Dove that nests on
sea cliffs. Our cities are now populated by large
numbers of pigeons descended from Domestic
Pigeons gone wild (feral). Their colours are
very variable. Basically seedeaters, they
eat bread and all kinds of
food scraps.

adult

Tawny Owl
(38 cm)
In woods, parks and gardens. Usually active at night, roosting hidden by day. Calls 'kee-wick' and also hoots. Nests in hollow tree. Eats mice, voles and other small mammals, also insects. Like other owls it brings up a pellet of undigested bones, fur and hard parts of prey.

young

Barn Owl
(36 cm)
Usually active at night, but may hunt at dusk. Found in many types of country, but especially farmland where it can nest in barns. Call an unnerving shriek. Eats mice, voles and rats, some birds, beetles and moths.

Little Owl
(23 cm)
Likes open country. Sometimes active by day, but hunts mainly at dusk and dawn. Does not hoot, but call is shrill. Nests in holes in trees, buildings or in the ground. Eats mainly insects, including beetles and craneflies, but some larger prey.

male

female

Kestrel
(34 cm)
Pointed wings. Male has grey head and tail. Lives on farmland, cliffs and moors, also seen in towns, and especially over motorway verges. Hovers in same spot watching for prey. Call shrill 'kee-kee-kee'. Nests on ledge or in hole. Eats mice, voles, and insects.

Buzzard
(55 cm)
In wooded areas, also moors and open country. Mainly in west in Britain. Soars on broad wings. Sometimes hovers. Mewing call. Makes nest of sticks in tree. Flying low, it pounces on rabbits and other small animals, including insects. Also eats carrion.

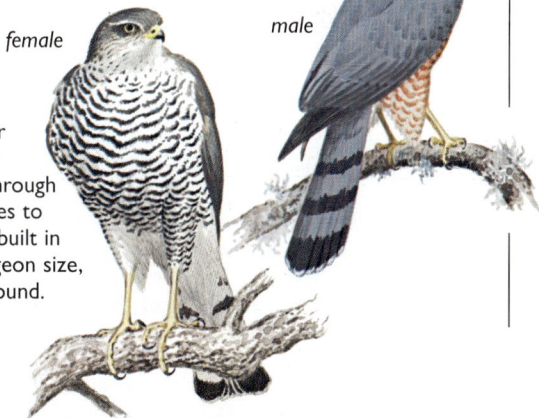

female

male

Sparrowhawk
(Up to 38 cm)
Male smaller but brighter colour than female. Flies fast on rounded wings through woodland or along hedges to surprise prey. Twig nest built in tree. Eats birds up to pigeon size, plucking them on the ground.

Pheasant
(84 cm male, 58 cm female)
Breeds wild, but large number bred
and released each year for shooting.
Found in farmland and woods. Takes
off with sudden commotion when
flushed. Nests on ground. Eats
seeds, leaves and insects.

female

male

Partridge
(30 cm)
In farmland and other open country
with cover. Often in families or
pairs. Nests in scrape on ground.
Eats grain, other seeds, leaves and
small animals.

Red-legged Partridge
(34 cm)
Found in farmland and heaths in western
Europe. Introduced to Britain, now
common. Nests on ground. Eats seeds
and leaves. Perches on walls and hedges.

Black Grouse
(53 cm male, 40 cm female)
Found in sparsely wooded fringes of moors and hills in Scotland and western England. Flight is strong and swift. Food varies seasonally and is mostly vegetarian. In spring, males compete ('lek') for females; in summer and early autumn, they moult. Nests on ground in thick herbage.

male

female

Red Grouse
(38 cm)
A colour variant of the Willow Grouse, which is found on moors and mountains in far north of Europe. Red Grouse found in British Isles on hill moors. Wings and body brown; slightly paler in winter, but no marked colour change. (Willow Grouse brown with white wings in summer, all white in winter.) Loud crowing call. Nests on ground. Eats heather shoots, other buds and berries.

Mallard
(58 cm)
Found in fresh water from parks to rivers, lakes and marshes. Sometimes at coast. Feeds at surface. Only female quacks, male has a quieter call. Nests on ground, usually near water. Eats mainly water plants, with some animal matter, which it sifts through fleshy fringes inside its bill. Like all ducks, male moults in winter to resemble female.

male

female

young

Tufted Duck
(43 cm)
On lakes and reservoirs. In winter may be in large flocks, and also along seashores. Dives underwater to find food. Fast flyer. Down-filled nest made close to water. Eats water plants, insects, small fish and frogs.

female

male

young

female

male

Pochard
(46 cm)
On lakes and slow-moving water. Most breed
in eastern Europe, coming to western Europe
including Britain in winter. Usually stay on water,
as walk poorly and need much effort to take off.
Dive for water plants and small animals to eat.
Wigeon looks similar, but grazes
around ponds rather than diving.

young

male

Shoveler
(50 cm)
Female similar to Mallard female.
Likes shallow muddy water,
where it can push its big bill
forward at the surface to sieve
out tiny animals and plants as food.

Teal
(35 cm)
Female speckled brown with green
wing patch. On small lakes and
ponds in summer, bigger areas of
water in winter. Fast flier. Nests on
ground in cover, sometimes away
from water. Feeds at surface. Eats
water plants and some small animals.
Very vocal: flocks chuckle or whistle
at all times.

male

red patch above beak   adult

young

Moorhen
(33 cm)
On ponds lakes, swamps and other places with waterside vegetation. Swims and walks well, with white tail jerking, but flight is weak. Nests on ground on platform of water plants. Eats insects, small fish and other animals, seeds, fruit and water weeds.

Coot
(38 cm)
Found on open stretches of water. Quarrelsome: fights with feet and wings. Jumps up as it starts a dive. Loud call of 'coot'. Makes nest of reeds above water, sometimes as a raft. Eats reeds, shoots, seeds, fish, tadpoles and insects.

white 'bald patch' on head

adult

juvenile   chick

Water Rail
(28 cm)
Lives in marshes and swamps,
and is shy: difficult to see amongst
the vegetation. Calls, including grunts
and squeals, may be heard from dense
reed beds at night. Nests above water
level on bed of dead reeds.
Eats insects, worms, freshwater
shrimps, roots, seeds and berries.

Spotted Crake
(23 cm)
Winter visitor or passage migrant in
south-east England. Lives in dense
swamps. Very shy and difficult to
see, but has loud calls, including one
like the crack of a whip, heard at
night. Flies weakly, with legs dangling.
Nests on boggy ground. Eats snails,
beetles and other insects, and seeds.

TERNS, with their slender bodies and forked tails, are sometimes called sea swallows. GULLS are more rugged birds; they are greedy feeders, and nest in colonies. All young gulls have mottled brown and white plumage in their first year. In the second year most gulls look like their parents, except for a black band on the tail. The Herring Gull takes five years to change from juvenile to adult plumage.

Common Tern
(36 cm)
Often called the 'sea swallow'. Summer visitor. Graceful flight. Dives to pick small fish from surface. Nests on sand and shingle beaches, on coasts and sometimes inland. A nesting colony dive-bombs intruders. Shrill call. Goes south in winter.

black tip to bill

Arctic Tern
(38 cm)
Very similar in appearance and habits to Common Tern, but slightly larger, with shorter legs and no black on the bill tip. Nests on coasts of northern Britain and Europe. Flies to Antarctic in our winter.

Herring Gull
(58 cm)
Very common. On coast and inland.
Yellow bill with red spot and pink
legs. Aggressive and noisy,
with loud yelping call.
Nests on ground, cliff ledges,
or sometimes buildings. Soars
and dives. Scavenges on rubbish
dumps. Eats refuse, shellfish, small
animals, eggs and young birds, including
young Herring Gulls.

immature

Great Black-backed Gull
(69 cm)
Huge. Very strong bill. Seen at coast,
rare inland. Nests on rocks, cliffs or
ground. Call low-pitched. Eats any
animals it can find dead or
overpower, including dead fish and
other carrion. Kills many young
seabirds.

Black-headed Gull
(38 cm)
Very common. Found at coast and inland. Sometimes follows tractors as they plough, feeding on small animals. Only has black head in summer. Nests in bogs, marshes and sandhills. Eats small fish, insects, worms, snails and scraps.

summer

summer

winter

young

winter

Kittiwake
(41 cm)
Yellow bill and short black legs. Usually stays far out at sea, but nests on cliff ledges, making a cup-shaped nest. Chicks stay in nest until they can fly. Name resembles its call. Eats fish.

chick

summer

winter

summer

chick

Common Gull
(41 cm)

Not actually common in Britain. Seen at coast and inland. Greenish yellow bill and legs. Nests on moors, marshes and shingle beaches in the north of Britain. High-pitched mewing call. Feeds on refuse, shellfish, worms, insects and other small animals.

Lesser Black-backed Gull
(53 cm)

Common on coasts, and also scavenges inland, often near industrial areas. Many move south in winter. British birds have dark grey back, Scandinavian birds are darker. Nests on cliffs and in cover on ground. Eats fish, shellfish, birds and eggs, carrion and refuse.

adult

chick

juvenile

Redshank
(28 cm)
Common wader in marshes and
meadows, and on coast in winter.
Three-note call. Nests on marshy
ground, hidden in vegetation. Eats
insects, worms and small shellfish.

Lapwing
(30 cm)
A wader, but usually seen on fields and
moors. Nests in scrape on ground,
following aerobatic spring display.
Sometimes called 'peewit' because of
the call it makes. Eats worms and
insects, especially farm pests such as
leatherjackets and wireworms.

Oystercatcher
(43 cm)
On coast, sometimes inland on moors and riversides. Noisy. Nests in scrape lined with shells and stones. Uses long bill to take food from rocks, break open shells and also to probe mud. Eats mussels and other shellfish, shrimps, crabs and worms.

Dunlin
(18 cm)
Common. Black below in summer only. Large numbers winter along British shores and mudflats. Fly in streaming, whirling flocks. In summer they go to moorland to breed in scrape nest lined with grass. Eats small animals, including insects and shellfish.

male

young

female

Mute Swan
(150 cm)
Male has larger black knob above bill
than female. On inland waterways
and lakes; sometimes on sheltered
sea bays. Nests on land close to
water. Protective of eggs and
young. Flies powerfully
after long take-off.
Wingbeat 'sings' loudly.
Eats water plants, and
a few animals.

female

juvenile

male

young

adult

Canada Goose
(100 cm)
As name suggests, introduced from
Canada to parks, but now widespread
on fresh water in Britain. Numerous
enough to be a pest in some places.
Lives in large flocks which graze on
grass and corn crops on land. Nest
hidden in vegetation near water.

young

Cormorant

(90 cm)
Found on coasts and estuaries, and
sometimes inland waters. Dives,
using its large feet to propel itself.
Often seen on rocks or posts with
wings outstretched to dry. Nest a
mound of seaweed on a rocky ledge
near the sea. Eats fish, especially
flatfish.

female

male

Heron

(90 cm)
Shallow water in wet meadows,
lakes, rivers and at the coast. Wades
and stands motionless as it watches
for prey. Stick nests built in colonies
in trees. Eats fish, frogs and water
voles.

male

Shelduck

(66 cm)
Large, goose-like. Sexes similar. Lives
on sandy or muddy coasts. Nests in
old rabbit burrows or other hidden
places. In midsummer, most British
adults fly to the German coast
to moult, leaving ducklings in
the charge of a few 'nursemaids'.
Mainly eats small animals such
as shellfish, crabs and insects.

Further Reading

Bailey, Jill, *Birds*. Eyewitness Explorer Series, Dorling Kindersley, 1996.
Burton, Robert, *Bird Behaviour*. Granada, 1985.
Lambert, Mike and Alan Pearson, *Letts Pocket Book of Birds*. Letts, 1993.
Peterson, Roger, Guy Mountford and P A D Hollom, *Field Guide to the Birds of Britain and Europe*. Collins, 1974 (3rd edition)
Royal Society for the Protection of Birds, *The Book of British Birds*. Automobile Association, 1994.

A good way to learn more about the animals and plants in your area is to join Wildlife Watch, a club for young people interested in wildlife and the environment. As well as organising activities for its members, Watch produces a national magazine, local newsletters, and many posters and activity packs. Their address is Wildlife Watch, The Green, Witham Park, Waterside South, Lincoln LN5 7JR.